# MANY VOICES

# Many Voices

## Andrew Oerke

Celestial Arts
Millbrae, Ca 94030

First Printing, October 1974
Made in the United States of America

**Library of Congress Cataloging in Publication Data**

Oerke, Andrew.
      Many Voices.

      I. Title.
PS3565.E7M3      811'.5'4      74-8285
ISBN 0-912310-60-X

# CONTENTS

Book I: A Voice . . . . . . . . . . . . 9
Introduction . . . . . . . . . . . . . . 13
The Voice of Man . . . . . . . . . . . 17
The Voice of Tireseus, Prophet of Thebes . 19
The Voice of Jesus . . . . . . . . . . . 21
The Voice of Buddha . . . . . . . . . 23
The Voice of Socrates . . . . . . . . . 25
Pythagoras . . . . . . . . . . . . . . . 27
Plato, The World of Forms . . . . . . . 29
Dante and Beatrice . . . . . . . . . . . 31
Antonio Porchia . . . . . . . . . . . . 33
The Return of Zuetzalcoatl . . . . . . . 35
The Voice of Black Elk . . . . . . . . . 37
The Voice of Montezuma . . . . . . . . 39
The Male, The Female . . . . . . . . . 41
The Voice of Age . . . . . . . . . . . . 43
The Voice of Language, One Man . . . . . 45
Book II: Abstracts . . . . . . . . . . . 47
The Voice of Silence . . . . . . . . . . 49
The Voice of Sound . . . . . . . . . . . 51
The Voice of Space . . . . . . . . . . . 53
The Voice of Time . . . . . . . . . . . 55
The Voice of Freedom . . . . . . . . . 57
The Voice of God . . . . . . . . . . . . 59
The Voice of Peace . . . . . . . . . . . 61
The Voice of Love . . . . . . . . . . . 63
The Journey . . . . . . . . . . . . . . 65
Book III: Voice of the Earth . . . . . . . 67
The Voice of the Earth . . . . . . . . . 69
I Heard the Many Voices of the Earth . . 71
The Voice of Winter . . . . . . . . . . 73
The Voice of Autumn . . . . . . . . . . 75
The Voice of Summer . . . . . . . . . . 77
The Voice of Fire . . . . . . . . . . . . 79
The Voice of Water . . . . . . . . . . . 81
The Voice of Air . . . . . . . . . . . . 83
The Voice of the Sun . . . . . . . . . . 85
The Voice of Night . . . . . . . . . . . 87
The Voice of the Mountain . . . . . . . 89
The Voice of the Lake . . . . . . . . . . 91
The Voice of the Forest . . . . . . . . . 93
Book IV: The Blending of the Voices . . . 95
The Voice of the East . . . . . . . . . . 97
The West . . . . . . . . . . . . . . . . 99
The North and the South . . . . . . . . 101
Postlude, the Four Homes of the Sun . . . 103
The Ten Commandments . . . . . . . . 105

# I

*A VOICE*

## A VOICE

If un-becoming is becoming,
    the flowers and faces that bloomed last year,
        the leaves through which the sun shone, and the vines
            of morning glory on the dawning trellis
                of another year are not memories only;
                    they are realities we must return to.

I watch the sun shimmering behind a veil
    of wind; I enter the velleities
        of leaves and feathers painted on the wind,
            the wind billowing its drapes across the sun,
            drawing me into rooms of memory
                and speculation, where I feel secure

and guarded and at peace – until the curtains
    drift again and experience recedes
        into the future and into the past
            with stunning velocity, and I both
            wrinkle and un-wrinkle into nothing
            I can recognize, until I am nothing

and the nothing is everywhere and everything,
    and the everything is nothing and nowhere.
        If the un-becoming is becoming.
            on the other side of the cutting edge
                of silence stands the gate through which whoever
                enters returns; whoever returns enters.

# INTRODUCTION

The difference of the voices is the sameness
of the voices as in Beethoven's Ninth,
in the quartet in which the variations
become the theme, the theme becomes the variations,
and the blending of the opposites becomes
at first insanity and then a higher
unity which is the ultimate in sanity.

The voices fly above the earth and burrow
in the earth; submerge themselves in waters
that are shallow, that are deep; or they arise
into the sky in feathered flight and song.
Each voice's phrasing leaves its signature
upon the air, and when one walks at last with death
the sum of all one's phrases is one's name.

# I
## *Dramatis Personnae*

*THE VOICE OF MAN*

*"Man goes nowhere. Everything comes to men, like the morning."*
*— Antonio Porchia.*

*Man goes nowhere and everything comes to him;*
  *man goes everywhere and nothing comes to him.*
    *How much our everything is really nothing;*
      *how much our nothing is really everything.*

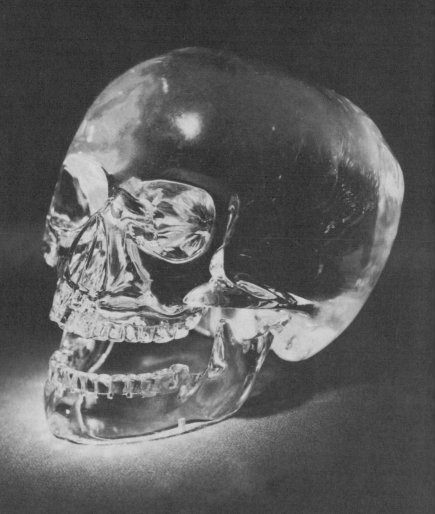

# THE VOICE OF TIRESEUS, PROPHET OF THEBES

*I Tireseus, blind and bereft,*
  *father and mother of situations which*
    *I never see fulfilled, which are never*
      *realized within the bosom of the present;*

*I Tireseus, tired and pregnant with*
  *knowledge, see the collapse of kingdoms*
    *and cities and cannot weep, for my eyes*
      *are dry. I Tireseus, old hag, male and*

*female for nothing, can yet rejoice*
  *that despite man's depredations there are leaves left;*
    *that in the helpless wailing yet a voice*
      *arises and begins to sing, and I listen.*

## THE VOICE OF JESUS

*I am not the one who you suppose I am,*
  *but my meditations have not been in vain.*
  *Enter my words if you would see to God.*
*Look in my eyes if you would know who I am.*

## THE VOICE OF BUDDHA

Many days I squatted under the bo tree
    wrapped in the warmth of my thoughts. The leaves became
        the stars, the stars became the leaves; the sun
            became the rain, the rain became the sun.

Many years I squatted under the bo tree
    wrapped in the warmth of no-thought: no reflections,
        no dreams, no imagery. The night became
            the day, the day became the night; day-night.

Many centuries I squatted under the bo tree
    wrapped in the warmth of the arms of the sky,
        wrapped in the warmth of the arms of the weather.

## THE VOICE OF SOCRATES

*"Crito, we owe a cock to Aesculapius. Pay it and do not neglect it." – last words of Socrates.*

*My thoughts are moving though my lips are still.*
*I feel the poison feeling for my heart.*
*I feel it squeezing where my life is frail.*
*I was judged to be an enemy of the state*
*even though I abided by all its laws.*
*Now that they hold the yearning of my heart*
*in their death-grip, I commend my life to God.*

## PYTHAGORAS

*Proportion is the harmony of life.*
   *The mysteries of architecture, music*
      *and geometry are of the same, seamless cloth,*
      *a certain relationship between*
         *certain numbers; this is the golden mean.*

*Each thing approximates ideal form.*
 *The idea that each thing manifests form,*
  *this, I see in retrospect, has changed*
   *the life of man by changing the forms of man.*

## DANTE AND BEATRICE

### DANTE

*I see a vision of my love, which becomes*
*a vision of the light, which becomes the whole light.*

### BEATRICE

*He stands before me with his arms outstretched*
*as if to embrace the light. When man and woman*
*come together in love a child is born.*
*Between us a common spirit is being born.*

## ANTONIO PORCHIA

*"We become aware of the void as we fill it." – Voices*

*We became aware of the voids as we*
  *fill it. Terror is the name of the game.*
    *Around ninety per cent of the body*
      *is water; about the same percentage of*
        *the mind is terror, or terror combined with awe,*
          *or terror preoccupied with its own*
            *survival. In the darkest recess of*
              *the mind the other ten percent is glass*
              *melting within the lenses of the eyes*
            *when terror turns to love. The rest of the while*
          *we shovel and shovel to fill the void,*
        *the abyss whose precipice we are afraid*
      *to look into, lest we become dizzy*
    *and drown in vertigo, the void which is within.*

33

## THE RETURN OF QUETZALCOATL

*I am returned to do away with colors,*
*all the colors of the rainbow. Let there be*
*no more colors; let all men be the color of man,*
*for each man's fate depends on all men's fate,*
*and all men's fate depends upon each one.*

# THE VOICE OF BLACK ELK

*Tree at the center of the Sacred Hoop*
*at the center of the earth, tree to bloom,*
*at last I see thy blossom, see thy boll.*
*At last my vision is not held in contempt;*
*at last my people are not held in contempt;*
*white man looks to red man to save himself*
*from himself; the movement has come full circle.*

*A prayer to the Earth that the Sacred Hoop may be known:*

*That it may bloom and fill with whistling birds,*
*that it may bloom and fill with tongues of song,*
*that it may bloom and fill with hands of praise,*
*that the Hoop may fill with a living flame,*
*that the Hoop may grasp with fingers of fire,*
*that the Hoop may hear its own sacred name*
*in the hearts and throats of its inhabitants.*

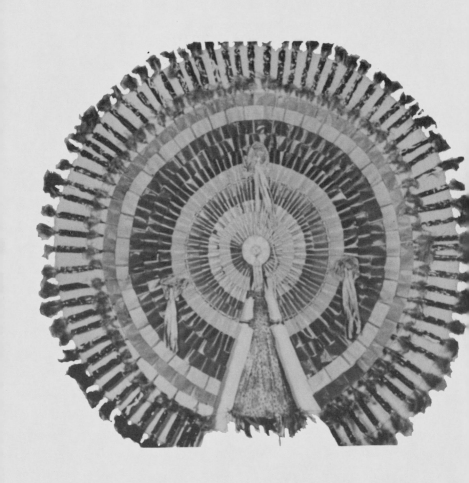

## THE VOICE OF MONTEZUMA

*"An age of battles more and, Lo! there remains the cross,*
*but not the priests; in their stead is FREEDOM and GOD."*
*—Montezuma's vision.*

*As I lay dying the spirit came to me*
*and opened the eyes of the future, saying,*
*"FREEDOM and GOD: Our only earth*
*will be the pyramid on which we worship*
*the mysteries and the beauties of the world;*
*in which we praise the coming in*
*and the going out of the seasons;*
*in which we glorify the leaf and the stem,*
*the eyelid and the palms as we would*
*the body and the mind of God Himself,*
*for each part and part of each is All."*

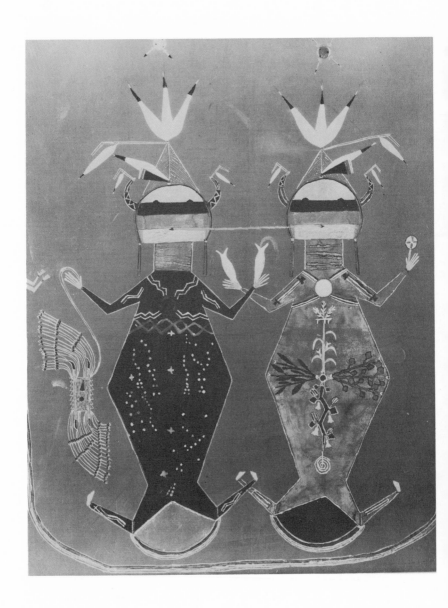

*THE MALE*

*A man is a forest in which one travels*
*to the other side of the woodland and into*
*the meadows of the plains country where light*
*forces the process of return, return*
*to the wandering, the darkness and the unknown.*

*THE FEMALE*

*A woman is a meadow flowing with light*
*and vistas that reveal other vistas*
*containing the fixed points of hearth and home.*
*A woman is a pasture brushed by wind*
*and light, in which we walk and plant our orchards*
*as we dwell among its blossoms, among its vines.*

*Beauty is not beauty unless it reveals*
*the inner form. According to an ancient legend,*
*under-thirty is not responsible for face.*
*After thirty, the art work starts to show*
*and every action is made manifest;*
*every thought and every action is proclaimed.*

*"Man, the one that thinks." – the dictionary.*

What do I mean when I say, "He is the one
   that thinks?" I mean he is the only one
   whose mind revolves full wheel to meet itself.
Man becomes mind and mind becomes man becoming.

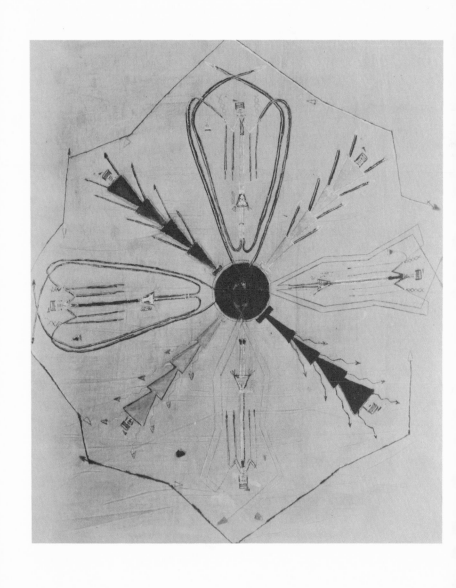

# II

*ABSTRACTS*

*THE VOICE OF SILENCE*

*I listen everywhere among the sounds*
   *both large and small of day and night; I hear*
      *the silent voices that one seldom hears.*
        *the rolling of the earth, rotation of*
           *the sun and stars, the music of the spheres.*

# THE VOICE OF SOUND

### 1.

The heavens open and a sound appears.
    The sound begins to shape itself an ear
that listens to the sound and spawns another ear.
    The purpose of the voice is to be heard.

### 2.

A sound is an event.
    In the beginning was the word
        and the word became speech
            and speech created the world
                in order to hear itself think.

### 3.

Still, the most lovely,
    most eloquent sound of all
        is the silence.

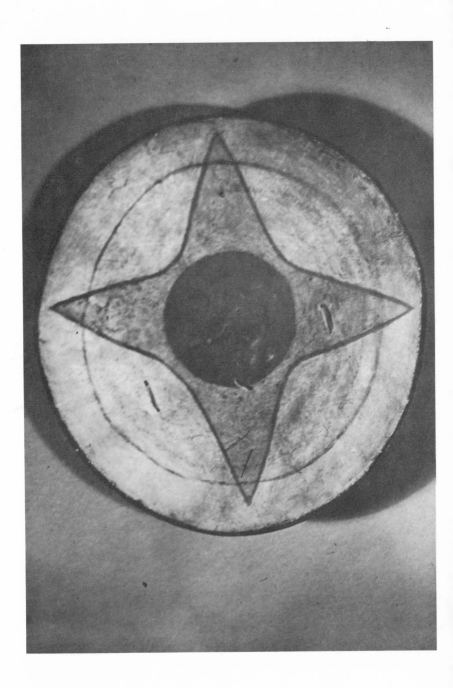

## THE VOICE OF SPACE

*Do not suppose that I am everywhere,*
*nor that I am everything to all men.*
*On the contrary, I am the particular,*
*the forms which waits to be perceived,*
*the figure lurking inside the marble,*
*and once I am perceived I have arrived.*

## THE VOICE OF TIME

*My voice is multifoliate like the branches*
*in the greenhouse you have built and nourished.*
*I do not exist except in process.*
*"Tick-tick," say the leaves, "tick-tick, time is green;*
*time is the anxiety of the unforeseen."*

## THE VOICE OF FREEDOM

*Freedom is un-freedom;*
*freedom is what is given up.*

## THE VOICE OF GOD

I AM WHO I AM EXODUS 3,14
I AM WHO I AM     I AM WHO I AM
I AM WHO I AM        I AM WHO I AM
WHO I AM I AM          WHO I AM I AM
I WHO AM AM I            I WHO AM AM I
AM I WHO I AM             AM I WHO I AM
I AM AM I WHO             I AM AM I WHO
I WHO AM I AM              I WHO AM I AM
I AM WHO I AM               I AM WHO I AM
I WHO AM I AM               I WHO AM I AM
I AM AM I WHO              I AM AM I WHO
AM I WHO I AM             AM I WHO I AM
I WHO AM AM I            I WHO AM AM I
WHO I AM I AM          WHO I AM I AM
I AM WHO I AM I        I AM WHO I AM I
I AM WHO I AM     I AM WHO I AM
I AM WHO I AM EXODUS 3,14

THE VOICE OF PEACE

I lie between the fields of summer and winter,
    a combination of the spring and of the fall;
I lie between the west wind and the east wind,
    between the north star and the southern cross.

I form the center of the Sacred Hoop,
    the line elliptical or curved that loops
and loops until it seals the sphere or spheroid
    that beats in the dove's heart and knows no fear.

*Before we talk about myself*
*I wish to say a word in my behalf:*
*If you have never drunk my wine,*
*if you have never felt my pain,*
*if you have never held me in your arms,*
*if you have never whispered in my ear,*
*if you have never wondered who I am,*
*if you have never wondered if*
*you could outlast my sleepless night;*
*if you have never looked into my eyes*
*you have never looked into your own eyes.*

# THE JOURNEY

*The voice of the journey and the journey*
*    itself are one and the same and hence one voice.*
*        There is no shorthand and no abridgement*
*            just as there is no short-cut and no by-pass.*
*                The path is the experience and the experience*
*            is the voice. Nor do I myself know*
*        what the voice will finally say to me;*
*    nor does the voice know where the path will end*
*since beginning is the end I could not anticipate.*

# III

*VOICE OF THE EARTH*

*THE VOICE OF THE EARTH*

*Touch my body as my touching bodies you,*
  *embraces you and lets you flow again;*
    *press my unassuming nakedness;*
      *return yourself to me as I return myself to you;*
        *journey with me as I journey with you*
          *through summer and winter, through spring and fall;*
            *revolve with me to the other side*
              *the sun and the other side of yourself.*
                *When day is done, voyage with me tonight*
                  *and moonlight; see the moon's face shining through*
                    *my leafy fringes and shadowy arrangements.*
                  *Touch me, take my hand; we shall walk*
                *where others have walked before and have left behind*
              *the essentials of their pretentions; walk*
            *with me where others have walked and hold me*
          *in your hand as my hands hold the holy flame of life.*

## *I HEARD THE MANY VOICES OF THE EARTH*

*I heard the many voices of the earth
   combine in unison as in the falling
      of water and the murmuring of wind.*

*I heard the many voices of humankind
   chanting in unison about the sun,
      the sound of their voices the sound divine.*

*I heard the many voices of the past
   return from darkness to surround the earth
      with melodies of vast simplicity.*

*I heard the many voices of the future
   turning backward so that we could hear
      the infinite regression of their song.*

*I heard the many voices in my cells
   assure me that the body is the soul
      though soul is more than mere addition of its parts.*

*I heard the many voices of the soul
   collaborating on a hymn of praise
      conspire to fashion LOVE and the world's new heart.*

## THE VOICE OF WINTER

*I fall into the arms of waiting earth.*
  *Though always flowing I am still the same*
    *design, the same energy and repose,*
      *and though "one never steps into the same stream twice"*
        *the same collection of waters within whiteness,*
          *the same whiteness you observed at your birth*
            *when your eyes opened and the light streamed through*
              *frosting the window of your mind with feathers of the swan.*

# THE VOICE OF AUTUMN

*I draw the winds of light into my arms;*
*I gather the winds of night into my arms;*
*I launch my leafy vessels into the air;*
*I celebrate the ripeness of decay,*
*the fallow mulch, the rich, rich reds and browns.*

*I am the mediation of extremes,*
*the consummation of your harvest dreams.*
*If you who watch me see me rise to fly*
*one fanning day into the atmosphere,*
*know, as I flow out of sight, that I go to other arms*
*for a dreamy season then I return.*

## THE VOICE OF SUMMER

*Season of leaf and leaf-light, sun in shadow*
*and without shadow, sun within you and*
*without you; gold on yellow, yellow on gold*
*in the shimmer and the shimmy of the sun.*

*Season of laundered nights when the moon mellow*
*shines and stars intersect the dome of sky;*
*I am the web of the sun and the moon*
*at the angle holding the strands of life in place.*

# THE VOICE OF FIRE

*My warmth preserves as it also destroys.*
*Listen to the dry rasping of my throat*
*and to the soaking hissing of my hands.*
*I am Shiva sacrificing the future and*
*the past reverently on the shrine of now.*

## THE VOICE OF WATER

*Flowing I flow into receptacles,*
*  and though I always change I never change.*
*    My rushing forward is returning to;*
*      returning to is also returning from,*
*        and rising from becomes the point of shift*
*          at which I fall again to free earth's forms.*

*I even am the mirror of myself.*
*  I sit beside a ledge and watch my fall*
*    fall as far as gravity will suck. I stay*
*      and go. I am the swaying to and fro*
*        whose paradox resolves itself within the whole.*

# THE VOICE OF AIR

*The voice I am is everywhere, a sucking round*
*the earth as my future self is formed and found.*
*A whirling of the light engenders death*
*and life, and in between them and above*
*and all around them flies myself, the breathing of*
*the earth, the turning inside-out of space*
*into low pressure and high, wind-thrust and counter-thrust.*

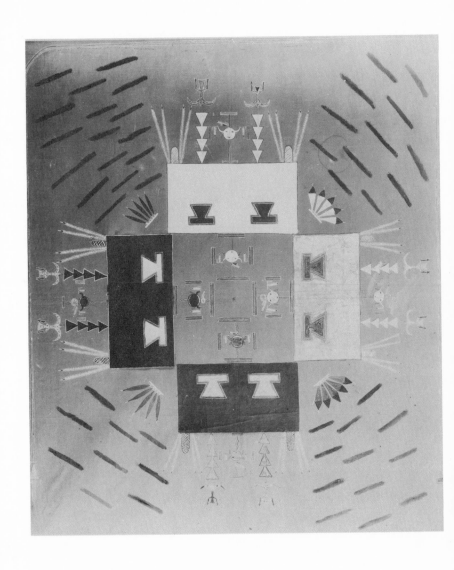

*THE VOICE OF THE SUN*

*I, Supreme Incan, strike the altar*
  *at the vernal equinox and on the bulky*
    *tablets of Stonehenge I announce the new year*
      *and then ascend the blue mountain of the air*
        *in my chariot scented with blossoms and plated*
          *with gold. I am the Incan Empire softening,*
            *melting and pouring its radiance beyond*
              *the Andean Hills into the oceans of night.*

## THE VOICE OF NIGHT

Quiet, quiet world of myself I give;
   quiet, quiet world of dark, interstellar
      space I give. The animals listen and know
         my ways. They sleep or pad without noise
            across my deserts and my plains, my woodlands
            and my mountains, my valleys and my heights.
         They patrol my body, preferring to live
      and to die in my gentler arms, my arms
that keep their secrets as a mother holds her child.

## THE VOICE OF MOUNTAIN

*A mountain is a mountain or a mountain*
*is a climb; or a mountain is a view*
*of itself or of the land around itself.*

*I begin where the level of the sea*
*leaves off; I leave off where the sky is thin.*

*The sky is the evaporation of the sea;*
*the sea is the condensation of the sky;*
*a mountain is the inversion of its cliffs.*

*The higher I toss the more likely it is*
*that if one ascends me one will also descend.*

## THE VOICE OF THE LAKE

*See and hear the forest in my throat,*
  *the lining of and shimmer of the leaves,*
    *the melody and keyboard of the wind,*
      *the eyes that browse at night while man's eyes dream,*
        *the eyes that peer into my depths and see*
          *inside themselves what lies behind themselves.*

## THE VOICE OF THE FOREST

My little brother, you who explore the stars
    with your fringing fingers and stretch the moon's
        web in your arms; my little brothers, you who
            explore the loamy subterranean vaults of
                earth with your long, searching tendrils, listen

to the prophecy of Black Elk, holy
    man of the Oglala Sioux, listen and hope:
        "In a sacred manner I have made him walk.
           The greening earth a pleasantness I make.
                The center of the nation's hoop I have made pleasant."

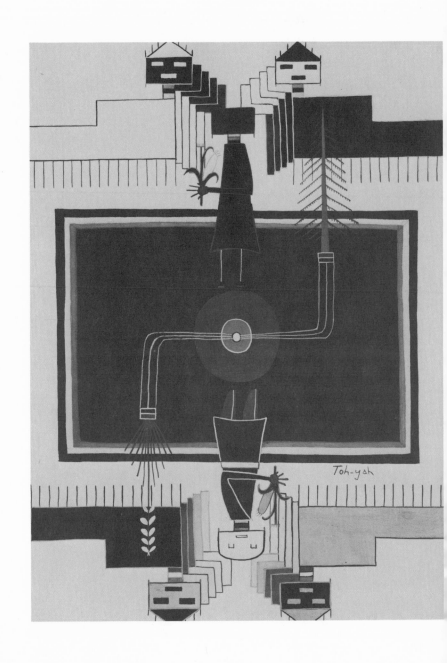

# IV

*THE BLENDING OF THE VOICES*

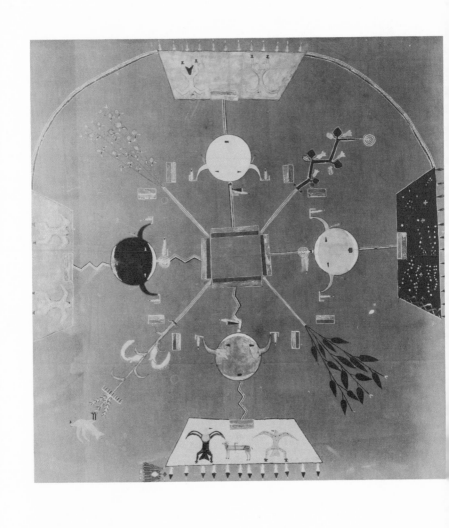

*The Voice of the East*

*In the East the East resides within one's heart;*
  *in the West one's heart resides within the West.*

*I see the East arising in the West,*
  *I see the West arising in the East,*
    *and now we each become the sparkle of*
      *the other as the light sparkles on the waves*
        *and the sea-waves sparkle in the light.*

                *\* \* \* \* \**

*I am as golden as my orient sun*
  *any my temples shining in the sun*
    *and my faces flashing in the sun*
      *like autumn leaves or tuna shaking off the hook.*

*I am also the mist of the morning*
  *and the evening dew, but my mind is moonlight,*
    *the shade and the moonlight, moonlight on the waters.*

                *\* \* \* \* \**

*I am the way in which the phrase is shaped,*
  *the sweep of elegance and courtesy*
    *by which my sense is known; the secret of*
      *the dragon's cave, the power of his voice.*

## THE WEST

*"As swift as the thought of me."* -- *Faust.*

*We face the universe continually*
*as our sphere spins on around the sun.*
*In the West a wind began to blow;*
*it sang the song of mine, the purity*
*of thought, the beauty of intelligent form.*
*The wind ignited a spark in man*
*and fires leapt from eye to eye, from tongue*
*to tongue until the culture was ablaze*
*and mind became the measure of all things,*
*until it, too, be purged upon the altar in the flame.*

### The North and the South

By traveling south eventually
   one travels north; by traveling north
      eventually the compass turns south.
         No matter in which direction one begins
            one's destination is the starting point.
            No matter what one's destination is
               one arrives at the point at which one began;
                  one begins at the point at which one ends.
                  The fate of the world and man's fate are one.

The northern lights reflect the arctic sun;
   the southern cross unfolds a hemisphere.
      The two spheres join within their opposites
         to be identical at their extremes
           of polar ice and equatorial steam.
            The world is one; its fate is undivided
            and indivisable. The seamless cloth
               of space surrounds earth's whirling like the weather,
               and like the weather, always changing, always
                is the same. " In our end is our beginning."

*Postlude, the Four Homes of the Sun*

*The four homes of the sun: East, West, North, South*
  *are also the four homes of the earth*
*in which the four races of man reside.*

*Inside the wigwam of the East I am the sun;*
  *inside the hogan of the West I am the moon;*
*inside the igloo of the North I shape the snow;*
  *inside the long house of the South I green the grass.*

*But there are ante-rooms; the central teepee*
  *is the heart of man in which the sacred fire burns:*
    *Here all are welcome, all a needed part*
      *of the seamless pattern in the mind of God,*
        *of the seamless fabric, which is the garment of God,*
      *of the individual, who is the face of God,*
    *of the winds, which are the eyes and ears of God,*
  *of the feelings, which form the heart of God,*
*of the thoughts, which make the consciousness of God,*
  *of one another, who are the love of God,*
    *of all of life, which is the song of God.*

## THE TEN COMMANDMENTS

### I

*Thou shalt become God, even as God has become you.*

### II

*Thou shalt become God and then thou shalt become man.*

### III

*Thou shalt remember every day to keep it holy.*

### IV

*Thou shalt honor every man as thou wouldst honor thy family and thyself.*

### V

*Thou shalt share what thou hast with thy neighbor.*

## VI

*Thou shalt make love; not war.*

## VII

*Thou shalt be pure in all thy thoughts and words and deeds.*

## VIII

*Thou shalt not judge others.*

## IX

*Thou shalt pray without ceasing.*

## X

*Thous shalt exercise thy body to keep it healthy, and thou shalt not abuse thy body nor thy neighbor's body.*

*XI*

*Thou shalt glorify God and cherish life.*


*XII*

*Thou shalt honor truth and knowledge.*


*XIII*

*Thou shalt not consider thyself inferior nor superior
to any other living thing.*


*XIV*

*Thou shalt not destroy nature or thou wilt destroy thyself.*


*XV*

*Thou shalt celebrate.*


*Let all of you become all of Me.*

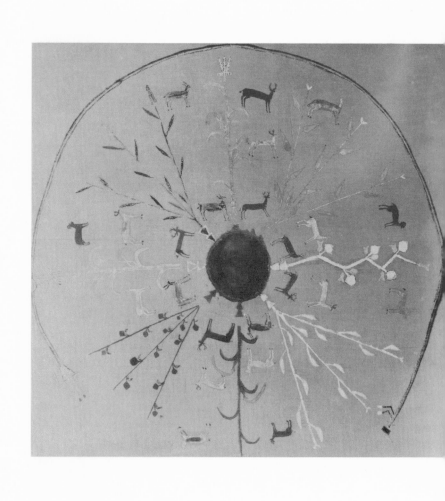

## List of Photographs & Illustrations

"Yesterday They Rode" . . . . . Flyleafs
Painting Titled Deer
    by Ma-Pi-Wi (Velino Shije) . . .Title Page
(Design Mandala) . . . . . . . . . . . . . 9
(Sun). . . . . . . . . . . . . . . . . . . 10
"Ceremonial Figure" . . . . . . . . . . 12
Indians in Council . . . . . . . . . . . 14
Osage Indian Girl. . . . . . . . . . . . 16
Rock Crystal Skull . . . . . . . . . . . 18
(diety) . . . . . . . . . . . . . . . . 20
Cast of Olmec Head . . . . . . . . . . 22
Carved Sandstone Human Face. . . . . 24
Cast Gold Musician . . . . . . . . . . 26
Member of the Fool Dance Society . 28
Guerrier Folle – Avoine. . . . . . . . .30
Tsagiglalal, The Guardian of Nohhlindih . 32
Plaster Cast of Quetzalcoatl . . . . . . .34
Memories . . . . . . . . . . . . . . . . 36
Man's Circular Headress . . . . . . . . 38
Altar for Male Shootingway.
    Earth and Sky . . . . . . . . . . . 40
(Old Indian) . . . . . . . . . . . . . . 42
Painting Titled Hopi Katchina
    by Fred Kaboti . . . . . . . . . . . 44
Altar for the Male Shooting Chant,
    or Navaho Windway. Cloud People. . .46
Canon Shadows . . . . . . . . . . . . . 48
Painting Titled Design: Tree and Birds
    by Ma-Pe-Wi (Velino Shije) . . . . . . 50
Painted Buffalo Hide Shield . . . . . .52
(Indian with Leaf Bonnet) . . . . . . . 54
Painting Titled Winter Dance
    by Tse Ye Mu . . . . . . . . . . . . 56
Prayer to the Great Mystery . . . . . . .58
Indian Tribal Ceremony . . . . . . . . 60
Aborigines of North America . . . . . . 62

Tribute to the Dead . . . . . . . . . . . 64
(Primitive Design) . . . . . . . . . . . 66
Bathing . . . . . . . . . . . . . . . . 68
"The Food Bearers" . . . . . . . . . . 70
"Dancer's Rendezous" . . . . . . . . . 72
Apache Reaper . . . . . . . . . . . . . 74
Arapaho Camp . . . . . . . . . . . . . 76
"Apache Fire Dance" . . . . . . . . . 78
Mandan Indian Village Across
    Missouri River . . . . . . . . . . . 80
Altar for Male Shootingway.
    Crooked & Straight Snake People . . . 82
Altar for Male Shootingway.
    Cloud Houses . . . . . . . . . . . . .84
Watching for the Signal . . . . . . . . 86
"Hearding of the Sheep" . . . . . . . 88
Bison & Elk on the Upper Missouri . . . 90
Ma-Pe-Wi (Velino Shije). . . . . . . . . 92
First Man, pine tree, and white corn;
    First Woman, yucca, and yellow corn. 94
Altar for Male Shootingway. The Skies . . 96
Custer's Monumental Sunset . . . . . . .98
Pizi or Gall . . . . . . . . . . . . . 100
(Totem Poles) . . . . . . . . . . . . 102
Cloth drawing showing sick man for
    whom ceremony is performed;
    medicine man; ceremonial dancer to
    represent deity; and woman, basket
    sacred meal . . . . . . . . . . . . 104
Altar for Plumeway. Game Animals
    and Plants . . . . . . . . . . . . .108

Photographs and illustrations used with permision from the Collection of the Newark Museum; the Library of Congress; the Museum of the American Indian, Heye Foundation; and, the Smithsonian Institute, National Anthropological Archives, Bureau of American Ethnology Collection.

I listen there everywhere among the sounds
both large and day of night; I hear
the silent voices one that seldom hears.
the rolling of the earth, with rotation of
the sun and stars, the music of the spheres.

THE ESSENCE OF ALAN WATTS. The basic philosophy of Alan Watts in nine illustrated volumes. Now available:

GOD. 64 pages, paper, $3.95

MEDITATION. 64 pages, paper, $3.95

NOTHINGNESS. 64 pages, paper, $3.95

THE HUMANNESS OF YOU, Vol. I & Vol. II. Walt Rinder's philosophy rendered in his own words and photographs. Each: 64 pages, paper, $2.95.

MY DEAREST FRIEND. The compassion and sensitivity that marked Walt Rinder's previous works are displayed again in this beautiful new volume. 64 pages, paper, $2.95.

ONLY ONE TODAY. Walt Rinder's widely acclaimed style is again apparent in this beautifully illustrated poem. 64 pages, paper, $2.95

THE HEALING MIND by Dr. Irving Oyle. A noted physician describes what is known about the mysterious ability of the mind to heal the body. 128 pages, cloth, $7.95; paper, $4.95.

I WANT TO BE USED not abused by Ed Branch. How to adapt to the demands of others and gain more pleasure from relationships. 80 pages, paper, $2.95.

INWARD JOURNEY Art and Psychotherapy For You by Margaret Keyes. A therapist demonstrates how anyone can use art as a healing device. 128 pages, paper, $4.95.

PLEASE TRUST ME by James Vaughan. A simple, illustrated book of poetry about the quality too often lacking in our experiences—Trust. 64 pages, paper, $2.95.

LOVE IS AN ATTITUDE. The world-famous book of poetry and photographs by Walter Rinder. 128 pages, cloth, $7.95; paper, $3.95.

THIS TIME CALLED LIFE. Poetry and photography by Walter Rinder. 160 pages, cloth, $7.95; paper, $3.95.

SPECTRUM OF LOVE. Walter Rinder's remarkable love poem with magnificently enhancing drawings by David Mitchell. 64 pages, cloth, $7.95; paper, $2.95.

GROWING TOGETHER. George and Donni Betts' poetry with photographs by Robert Scales. 128 pages, paper, $3.95.

VISIONS OF YOU. Poems by George Betts, with photographs by Robert Scales. 128 pages, paper, $3.95.

MY GIFT TO YOU. New poems by George Betts, with photographs by Robert Scales. 128 pages, paper, $3.95.

YOU & I. Leonard Nimoy, the distinguished actor, blends his poetry and photography into a beautiful love story. 128 pages, cloth, $7.95; paper, $3.95.

I AM. Concepts of awareness in poetic form by Michael Grinder. Illustrated in color by Chantal. 64 pages, paper, $2.95.

GAMES STUDENTS PLAY (And what to do about them.) A study of Transactional Analysis in schools, by Kenneth Ernst. 128 pages, cloth, $7.95; paper, $3.95.

A GUIDE FOR SINGLE PARENTS (Transactional Analysis for People in Crisis.) T.A. for single parents by Kathryn Hallett. 128 pages, cloth, $7.95; paper, $3.95.

THE PASSIONATE MIND (A Manual for Living Creatively with One's Self.) Guidance and understanding from Joel Kramer. 128 pages, paper, $3.95.

$3.95

# THE VOICES OF TIME

Tiresias, prophet of Thebes; Jesus; Buddha; Socrates, and Pythagoras speak through the ages through Oerke. Plato returns to manifest his ideals through a new poetic form, Dante and Beatrice speak again. Oerke has chosen his dramatis personae carefully, and the words he has chosen to represent them echo in the mind long after the book is closed. For *Many Voices* Oerke has chosen illustrations chiefly drawn from mythological themes of American Indians. These brilliant reproductions, used with permission of various museums, the archetypes which Jung described are applied to illustrate themes that are limited by neither time nor space.

CELESTIAL ARTS
MILLBRAE, CALIFORNIA